A COMPLETE STEP-BY-STEP GUIDE TO STENCILLING

The Stencilling Studio

JANE WILDGOOSE

First published in Great Britain in 1994 by
Chancellor Press
an imprint of Reed Consumer Books Limited
Michelin House, 81 Fulham Road
London SW3 6RB
and Auckland, Melbourne, Singapore and Toronto

Production Controller: Victoria Merrington
Executive Editor: Judith More
Art Director: Jacqui Small

Produced, edited and designed by Blackjacks Ltd, London
Photography: Mark Gatehouse
Colour Origination: Scanners

This product is suitable for ages 14 years upwards.
We recommend that children under the age of 14 years should be supervised by an adult.

Not suitable for children under 36 months.

ISBN 1 85152 648 X

Printed and bound in China
Produced by Mandarin Offset

Contents

Introduction

Stencils are wonderfully versatile and have been used for centuries to enhance a wide variety of surfaces. Only quite simple equipment and techniques are required and the materials need not be expensive. All these factors make stencilling a very rewarding and economical way of enhancing a room or a piece of furniture or clothing.

It is worth making sure that surfaces to be stencilled are properly prepared before you commence. Fabric should generally be washed and ironed according to its fibre content; walls should be cleaned and filled before painting; furniture should be filled if necessary and any varnish or old paint removed with the appropriate solvent according to the manufacturer's instructions, then sanded and cleaned. These preparations may seem frustrating when you want to get on with the creative business and see a result, but a little time spent at first will make the time you spend decorating that much more rewarding, as the effects will be more durable.

Time should be spent, too, at the end of the decorating to make sure that the stencilled fabric is fixed properly so that it is not effected by washing and light. Painted stencils on furniture and floors should be sealed with appropriate varnish, with a minimum of 2–3 coats (more on areas of hard wear – floors, for instance). Be sure to sand between each coat of varnish or it will flake with wear, and to clean up all traces of dust after each sanding. It may seem laborious, but it really is worth the trouble. Varnish must, of course, be applied to the whole surface, not just the stencilled area.

Many different paint types can be used and it is worth experimenting with various types, as most people end up having favourites which work in ways that seem best to them. Matt or shiny effects can be tried, as well as experimenting with painting your own backgrounds: on fabric, or making stippled, sponged, grained or marbled effects on walls or furniture. Colour, texture and finish will all dramatically affect the way the stencil finally looks. You might like to try some small experiments with the stencils to see how combinations of bright, contrasting colours, tone on tone, or dark, sombre colours affect the results. You should also try to develop some ideas about the effects you will eventually want to create when you come to make your own stencils.

PAINTS

Virtually any paint can be used for stencilling, although those which are quick drying are the most practical. Emulsion paint has been used for two of the projects in this book. It is now available in an enormous range of colours and some of the major paint manufacturers supply 250ml tester tins in matt finish which provide the beginner with literally hundreds of inspirational, exciting colours from which to choose at low cost. Browsing through the colour charts, mixing and matching shades, can suggest colour ideas you might not have considered if you had to mix the colours yourself.

If you are already confident about using and mixing colours, then you may wish to experiment with making up your own colours. Acrylic paint thinned with water and a little PVA, artists' pigments sold in powder form (not to be confused with pigments for textile use) can also be mixed with water and PVA, or signwriters' colours, are all widely used. All these finishes will

need to be sealed with the appropriate varnish. Oil- and alkyd-based varnish available in matt and gloss finishes, are suitable for most paint types, but may yellow considerably with age. PVA or acrylic varnish are water-based and can be used over emulsion or acrylic finishes. Polyurethane varnish is extremely tough and

particularly appropriate for areas of really hard wear, like floors. It is also available in matt or glossy finishes. Professionals often keep certain brushes only for use with varnish. Make sure you always wash brushes out immediately after using varnish, with the appropriate solvent – particularly when using oil, alkyd or polyurethane varnishes, when white spirit is required – if you do not want to end up with solid brushes which can no longer be used.

A compass is useful for circular motifs, but it is possible to improvise with other round objects: e.g. a cup or a roll of tape.

Small stencil brushes are ideal for fiddly details.

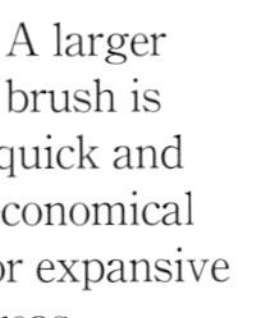

A larger brush is quick and economical for expansive areas.

For applying colour to fabric, special pigments are available; these are usually called fabric paints and are characterized by manufacturers' instructions to fix them by ironing. Available ready-mixed in small containers, these colours can be mixed together; they have a consistency not unlike thick emulsion paint, making them reasonably easy to handle. They are water soluble until dry, and further fixed to the effects of washing and light by ironing. They will work on nearly all fabric surfaces. Dyes can be used for stencilling on fabric, but unless a spray is used they need to be thickened with appropriate thickener (Manutex or ready-prepared) and will need to be steamed for fixing, precluding their use on large areas such as curtains, unless you have access to a professional's steamer. Care must also be taken to choose the right dye for the fabric on which you are working.

Textile stencil cream provides an ideal texture for stencilling on fabric, being crumbly, and it will work on most fabrics. It does take quite a long time to dry completely, which can present problems if you are working on a large piece of cloth (such as curtains) in a small area where you need to move the fabric repeatedly.

OTHER EQUIPMENT

In addition to the equipment and materials discussed later in the sections on making stencils (stencil paper, craft knife, tracing paper, pencil, eraser, ruler, graph paper, masking tape, compass and protractor) and techniques (brushes, roller, sponge, spray), you will need a protective

Scissors are used for trimming stencil paper to size.

A sharp craft knife is essential for accurate stencil cutting, but great care must always be exercised in its use. *Never* cut towards your free hand or body.

This type of little foam roller is a quick and economical way of blocking-in stencils.

apron or overalls, depending on the scale of your work, and rubber gloves, which should always be worn if your hands will come into contact with paint or textile colours. A vapour mask is a valuable addition for use with sprays or varnish, and you should always work in a well-ventilated room when using these materials.

Plenty of newsprint, or old newspapers, are invaluable for masking areas or keeping other surfaces clean while you work. Old pieces of rag for mopping up will be needed, too. Cheap enamel plates make ideal palettes for mixing small amounts of colour.

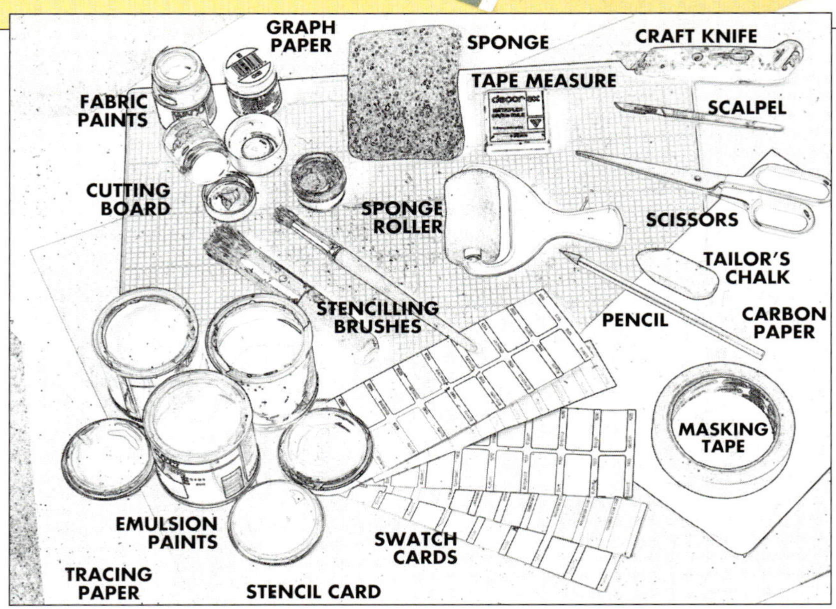

MAKING YOUR OWN STENCIL

Inspiration for making stencils can be found in all sorts of decorative sources: old and new textiles, china, tiles, style magazines and so on. All provide a rich source both of ideas and colour combinations which can be adapted to your own taste.

Most ideas will need to be modified in order to fulfil the particular requirements of stencil cutting. The patterns will need to be worked out in such a way that separate elements remain joined together, at least by a small link or 'tie' of stencil paper. Opinion is divided about whether these links should subsequently be painted in, making a smooth unbroken line or left as a characteristic part of the design. It is up to the individual and you will probably make up your own mind when you start to design your own stencils.

LAYING OUT A STENCIL

When you have chosen a design,
make a sketch on paper and work out
where you will need to make 'ties'.
Some designs are very simple and
they will not be needed. Others are
more complicated and then it helps to
shade in the areas which will be cut
out. You can then see more easily if
you have missed the positioning of a
'tie', needed to prevent a piece of the
design dropping out of the stencil
paper when it is cut.

The design illustrated (used in
the *Floor Border* project) was inspired
by a very small area of a wallpaper
border. Because it has straight lines
which need to be joined up from one
stencil area to the next, it was first
drawn up on graph paper. It is
extremely important to be accurate
when repeating straight lines or they
will not join up properly from one
stencilled area to the next. It helps to
make them broken, too, as joins are
difficult to achieve, and mistakes look
much more noticeable when repeated
at regular intervals.

Geometric shapes like the *Star*
are much easier to work out on graph
paper, too, and the distances between
them for the repeat can easily be
measured accurately. More fluid or
naturalistic designs would be better
worked out on plain paper. If you
particularly like using geometric
elements, a small geometry set with
compass and protractor is invaluable,
although you can easily improvise by
drawing round objects such as cups
and saucers.

When the design is ready, transfer
it on to tracing paper using a soft (2B)
pencil for the first tracing and a harder
(HB) pencil to transfer the design. You
can use carbon paper to transfer the
tracing, but this tends to smudge when
you are cutting out. If the tracing on
the stencil paper is rather faint then
go over it again with the 2B pencil.

371
368

CUTTING A STENCIL

Cut the stencil with a sharp craft knife, taking care always to cut away from your free hand and your body. *Never* cut towards you in case the knife slips. A cutting board of the type sold by graphic artists' suppliers is an ideal surface on which to work, but they are expensive, and an old piece of ply or hardwood larger than the size of your work is quite adequate.

Standard stencil paper is extremely good to use as it is specially treated to resist absorbing too much paint. It is quite expensive, though, so do be sure you are absolutely happy about your stencil before you start to cut. Clear, hard plastic (acetate) can be used, but it needs to be wiped down regularly when you are applying the colour, since more seepage can occur. Strong brown wrapping paper painted with shellac and then allowed to dry makes a good, cheaper alternative.

When the stencil is all cut you are ready to start applying colour. It is a good idea to wipe stencils down over a piece of newsprint if they get clogged with paint during use (make sure no wet paint is trapped on the underside before re-using). When you have finished work, wipe the stencil down thoroughly and leave to dry, then store flat. (You will have great difficulty in getting them to lie flat after they have been stored, rolled or folded.) It is worth keeping your stencils properly; you will have spent a lot of time and care in making them and you may well want to use them again in the future.

APPLYING COLOUR

Many different effects can be achieved when applying colour with stencils. Tones of colour can be built up in layers or colours can be blended into one another. You may find that it is helpful to practise applying colour before starting the projects to get some idea of the effects that you prefer and would like to achieve.

When applying a light colour over a dark background (as in the *Dado Frieze* project) you will find that the background colour affects the purity of the lighter colour applied over it. You can choose to nullify this effect by first stencilling in white. When the white is dry apply the lighter colour (this method is particularly appropriate if you are aiming for a fairly flat, even effect). Alternatively, as in the project, you can lay the light colour directly over the dark painted ground, allowing some of the background colour to show through, giving a more mottled, lighter-weight effect. Experimentation on small pieces will allow you to discover your own favoured methods of applying colour, whether for flat, even results or mottled, blended effects.

Various effects can be achieved by using different types of equipment to apply the colour. Shown here are the four methods of application most often used. They are demonstrated on calico with pigment for textile use (Dylon Color Fun Soft Fabric Paint was used), but are equally appropriate for use with all kinds of paint finishes and on many different surfaces.

You will find that some methods of application are more economical than others or suit you better. Aerosol sprays seem quick and easy, but the kind of paint generally sold in aerosol cans has very unpleasant (and frequently inflammable) fumes and should not be used without wearing a vapour mask and working in a well ventilated area: the fumes tend to linger quite a long time. However, dye or textile pigment mixed with water can be sprayed on to fabric and can be very effective for a faded, distressed look on velvet. It is generally a matter of choosing the technique that best suits your requirements.

Using a Stencil Brush

Using a special stencil brush with firm bristles all of the same length is probably the most common way of applying stencil colour Only take up a little colour on the very end of the bristle and dab off any excess before you start. If you apply too much colour the effect will look rather clogged and heavy. It will also be less economical. Use a light, dabbing motion and experiment with leaving some of the background showing through, building up to darker tones and also with blending colours. You might like also to experiment with a large and a small brush. The larger brush will give a lighter effect, but you may find it a little more difficult to control on more intricate areas.

Using a Sponge

Using a sponge is a very economical method and gives a distinctive mottled effect. If the sponge is new, rinse it in water and squeeze out thoroughly before dipping into the colour.

As with the brush, only take up a very small amount of colour, dab off excess before you start and use a light, dabbing motion. Colours can be blended extremely successfully with a sponge, either in one coat, blending as you go, or in layers which are left to dry after each colour is applied.

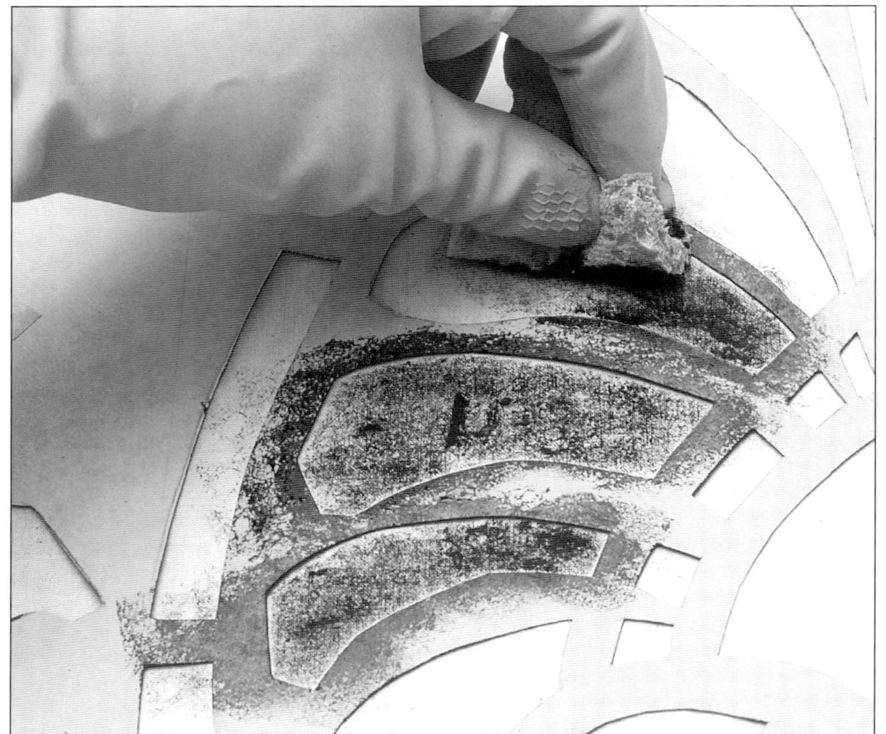

Using a Roller

Using a small foam-sponge roller is probably the most economical method of achieving fairly dense, even coverage, especially on fabric, which absorbs the colour quite rapidly when it is applied with a brush. This little roller was purchased in a toy shop, but is ideal.

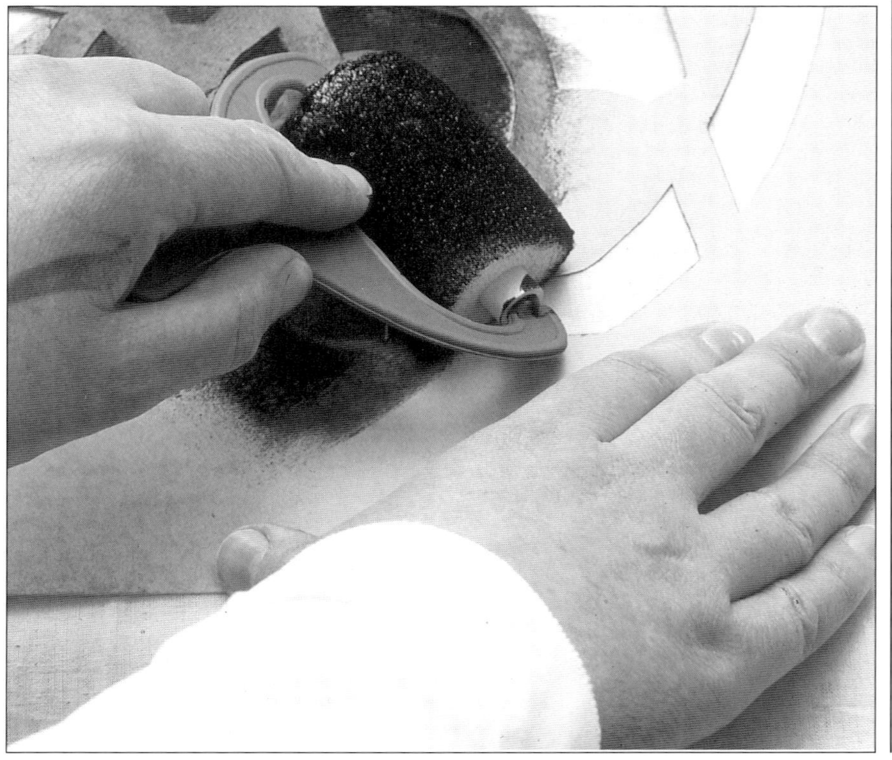

Aerosols

Aerosols are frequently recommended for use with stencils, but their use is not always ideal. Not only can the fumes be a problem (see page 13) when using commercial aerosol paint spray, but a great deal of careful masking with newsprint is essential if you do not want inadvertently to spray the surrounding area; spray can travel quite a long way outside the stencil. Seepage of paint under the edges of the stencil can be a problem, too. However, sprays are wonderful for laying large areas of flat colour and this may be just what you want for a particular project. Sprays can be particularly effective when used on fabric. Textile pigment is the easiest, as it only has to be ironed to fix it. Mix with water, about 1:1, and put in a plant spray. Dye can be mixed with water and used in the same way, but it will, of course, have to be the appropriate dye for the fabric you are using and it will have to be fixed by steaming. Always wear a mask when using sprays for stencilling.

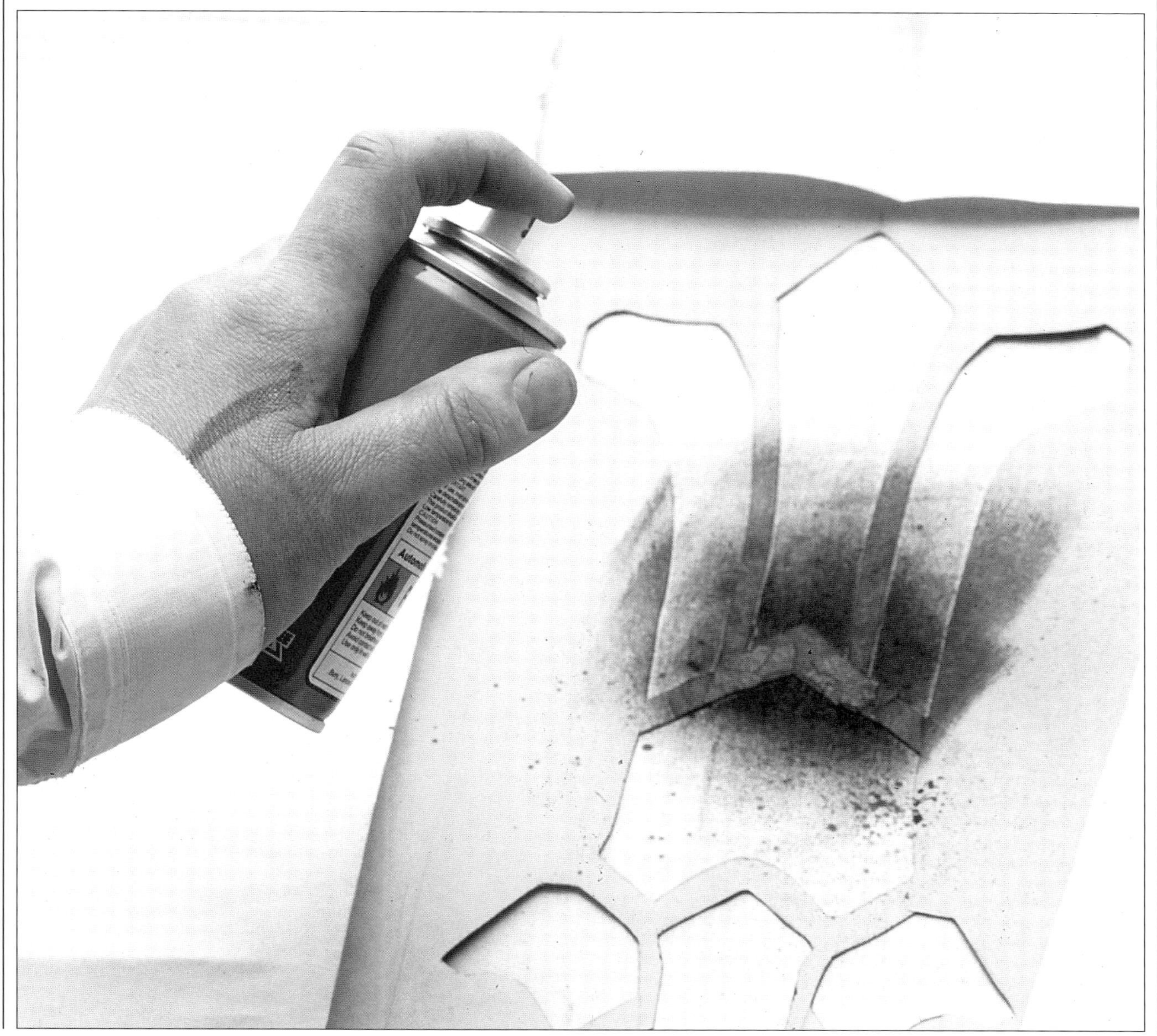

STAR AND LEAF DESIGN

Stencilling on furniture is a traditional way of making a poor-quality or plain piece more interesting. With simple, bold motifs, junk-shop finds and standard mass-produced furniture can be customized to go with a room scheme. Paint left over from decorating can be used up, or contrasting colours can be chosen, depending on your taste, to give the most bland or damaged piece a new life.

This motif was taken from a repeating wallpaper design of 1810 and simplified to make a colourful design for the side of a small cupboard. It has been designed to fit the dimensions of a fairly standard cupboard, but could be enlarged or reduced as required.

Stencilling on furniture is usually associated with small, rustic floral patterns and often muted or sludgy colours. This design is deliberately made bold and bright. The colour is applied with a brush and made quite even for maximum colour contrast. Because the background is lighter than the colour stencilled over it, this is easy to achieve with one coat.

This particular design was very simple to translate into a stencil because none of the separate elements fall too close together, and there are no long, straight lines; therefore the linking sections or 'ties' which hold together intricate patterns on stencils were not a consideration. When designing your own stencils, particularly at first, simple patterns like this can be very rewarding, as they look convincing but do not require too much competence!

1

1 The background was painted with Dulux Matchmaker matt emulsion 1181 'Daffodil'. The dimensions of the cupboard side were drawn up on the front of the stencil in pencil to make it easier to position centrally. Once in position, secure the stencil with masking tape.

Apply Dulux Matchmaker matt emulsion 1239 'Glade' with a small stencil brush on the details. This helps to control unwanted paint seepage under the edge of the stencil.

2 Continue with the small brush round the inner edge of the star shape.

3 Fill in the centre of the star with a large stencil brush, blending the colour into the paint already applied (the colour will appear darker around the edge where paint has already been applied).

N.B. When using emulsion on furniture it should be sealed when thoroughly dry with an appropriate varnish; alternatively, when decorating woodwork, use eggshell or one of the other paint finishes designed for wood, but remember these take much longer to dry and are messier.

4 This design – extremely simple but very eye-catching – could be used on a table top, or the seat of a chair; it could be reduced and repeated all over a small piece of furniture, or applied to the centre of a plain ceiling in place of a ceiling rose. Very often the simplest designs can be most effective, depending on use of colour for their effect.

HOLLY MOTIF

Children derive great pleasure from giving and receiving cards, and generally enjoy making their own. Stencilling is an ideal medium whereby even quite small children can use simple techniques to produce results they can be proud of. Obviously an adult must cut the stencils, as the sharp craft knife necessary for cutting the stencil paper would be far too dangerous in small hands, but once they are cut, the designs can be very quick and easy to reproduce. Christmas motifs lend themselves especially well to this medium: Christmas trees, holly and ivy, stars, and so on, are all appropriate, since they have strong silhouettes and are clearly recognizable without the addition of fiddly details.

The simplest sprig of holly was used as the motif for this project. The stencil could also be repeated several times on a sheet of stencil paper (see the *Fleur-de-lys* project on page 38 for putting a motif into repeat) or repeated at random to decorate wrapping paper as well. Plain red, green, gold or silver paper would all be very effective as backgrounds, both for wrapping paper or for the card. Frequently, very simple stencils are greatly enhanced by the colour of the background to which they are applied.

Artists' acrylic colours are used here; powder paint mixed to a fairly thick consistency, poster paint, or any other water-based paint can be used. Children's non-toxic, washable paints are highly recommended for small children; and, of course, suitable protective clothing should be worn.

1 Allowing at least a 1 in. (2.5cm) border around the edges of the stencil, cut pieces of card large enough to fold in half. Make sure the stencil is positioned correctly and then secure with a small piece of masking tape at each corner.

2 Colour can be applied with a sponge or brush. Care should be taken not to apply too much colour at once; excess paint can be dabbed off on a spare piece of paper. It is simplest to put the red and green paint on separate saucers or enamel plates so that the colours do not get mixed by mistake. Using a separate sponge for each colour will help avoid this problem too.

Apply the green to the leaves; a little black or darker green can be blended into this to give depth. White can be added to provide highlights.

3 Finally, add the red paint to the berries and allow to dry sufficiently so that the stencil can be removed without smudging the design.

4 Unpeel the masking tape and discard, then lift the stencil straight up to reveal the finished effect.

Further embellishments can be added: a Christmas greeting could be stencilled, written, printed with a child's printing set, or applied with letraset.

Simple, yet striking, designs like stars can be applied with a stencil using children's glue. The glue is applied through the stencil and left until it is tacky. Then the stencil is removed and glitter sprinkled over to give a slightly more sophisticated variation to an old favourite.

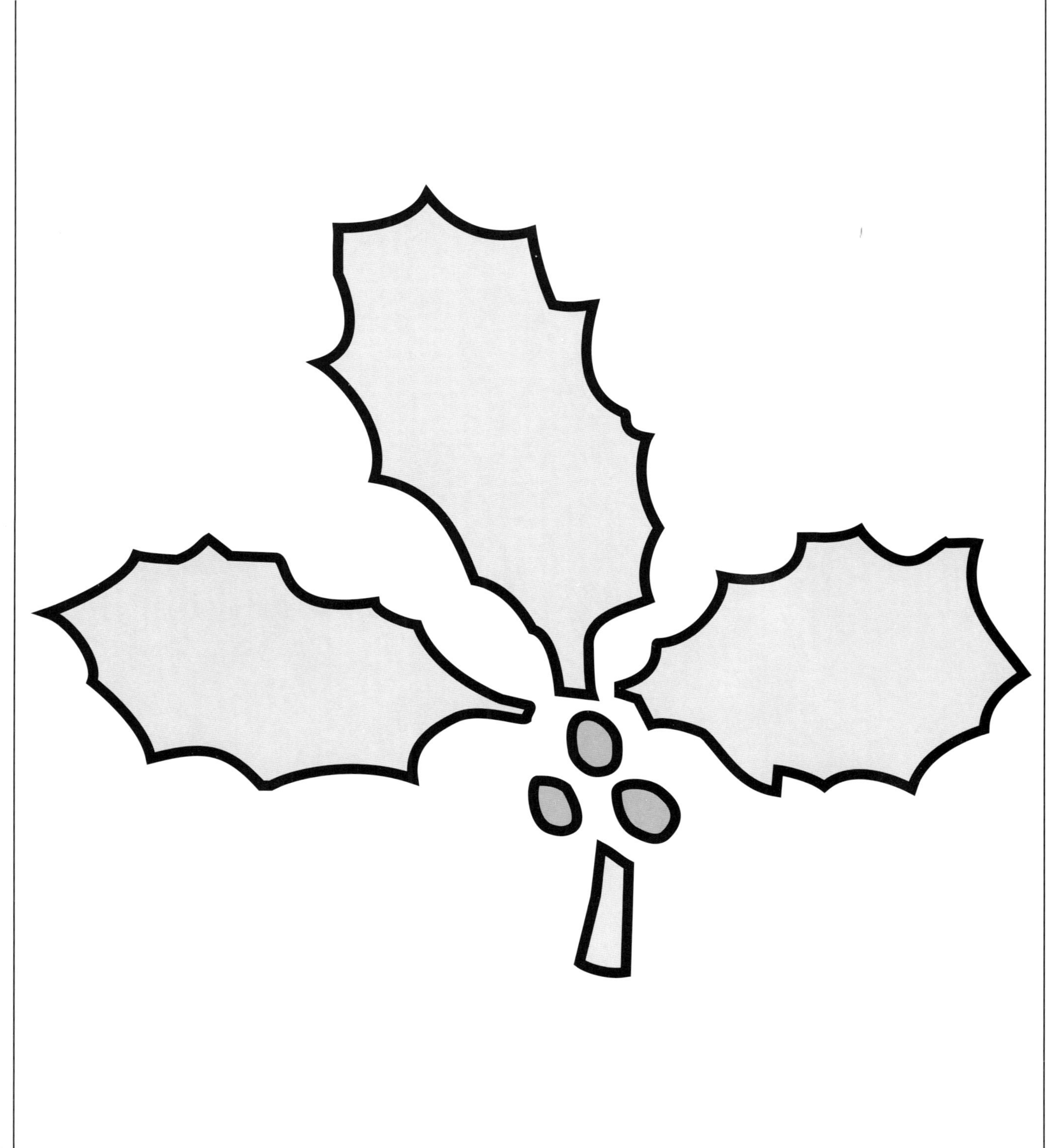

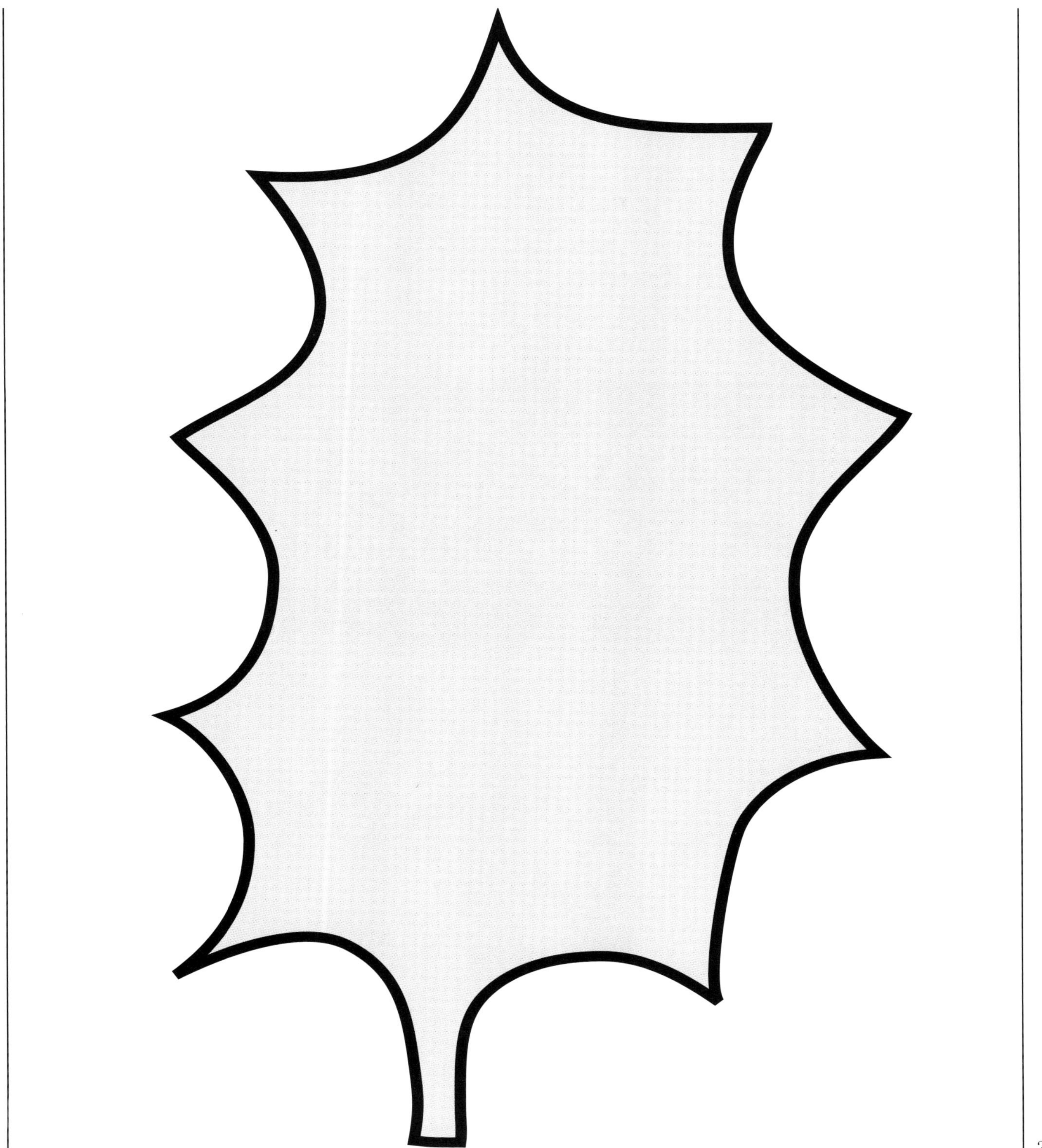

STARS AND TRIANGLES IN BLACK

If the idea of bold, bright, large-scale patterns on furniture or walls seems too heavy for your taste, but you want to add a distinctive touch to an otherwise plain and simply furnished room, a stencil border on a sanded or plain-coloured floor can be very effective. Alternatively you may become so enthusiastic about the design that you feel inspired to include every surface in it. Either way, a stencilled border on the floor is an ingenious way of finishing off a room and need not be too complicated, particularly if you were planning on varnishing the floor anyway.

This design was taken from a detail on the border of a more elaborate design (*shown below*) – with a fair amount of 'artistic licence' employed.

Straight lines are always a problem on repeating stencil patterns as they need to be drawn out very accurately so that they will join up properly in repeat, without going off at an angle. The simplest way to achieve this is to draw up the design on graph paper before transferring it onto the stencil paper by tracing. Graph paper makes all geometric designs simpler to plan.

Long straight lines can be a problem, too, if cut close together, as they make the stencil flimsy and difficult to handle; joins will inevitably show up at regular intervals as darker areas if overlaps occur. To avoid these problems the straight lines were separated with uncut 'ties' at regular intervals, forming part of the design. For this project aerosol paint has been used for a slightly different effect, but any of the other methods of applying colour could be employed, particularly if you prefer not to work with materials with strong fumes.

1 Measure, and mark at regular intervals from the edge of the wall so that the stencil can be positioned exactly parallel with it. A small, light pencil mark can be used and then a small piece of masking tape laid down for lining up the stencil. This avoids making obtrusive marks on the floor; a piece of tape at either end of the stencil is sufficient to get it straight.

2 Using newspaper or newsprint, mask all the areas around the stencil, including the wall. Take care not to forget the area between the stencil and the wall. Shake the aerosol thoroughly and apply a light coat of spray from approximately 10–12 inches away. Leave to dry thoroughly. Work in a well ventilated area and wear a vapour mask.

3 Lift the stencil and line it up with the pattern on the floor, overlapping the last two elements on the end of each line. Secure the stencil. A little double-sided tape on the reverse side of any details which are reluctant to lie flat will help to avoid paint seeping under the edges of the stencil.

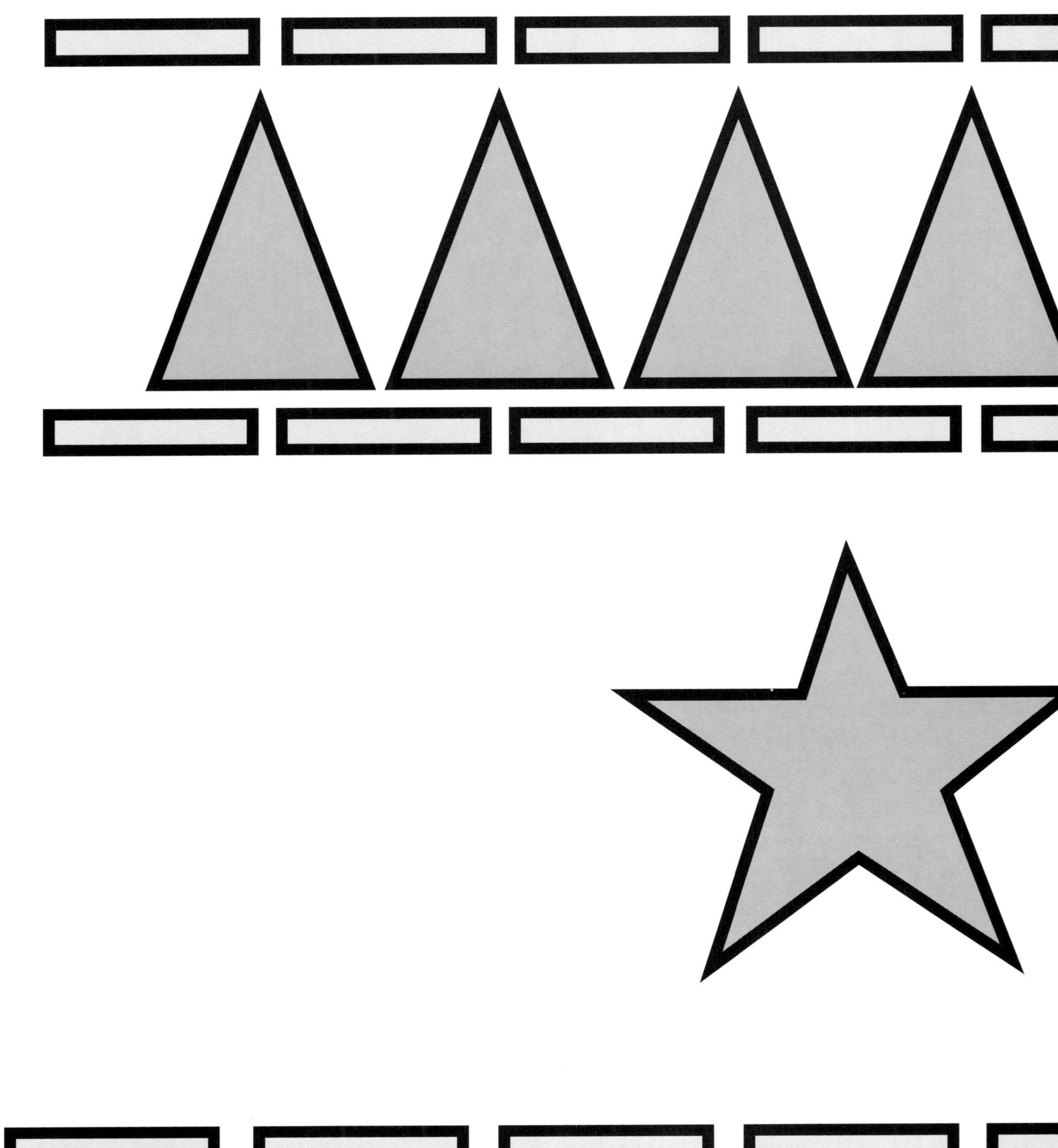

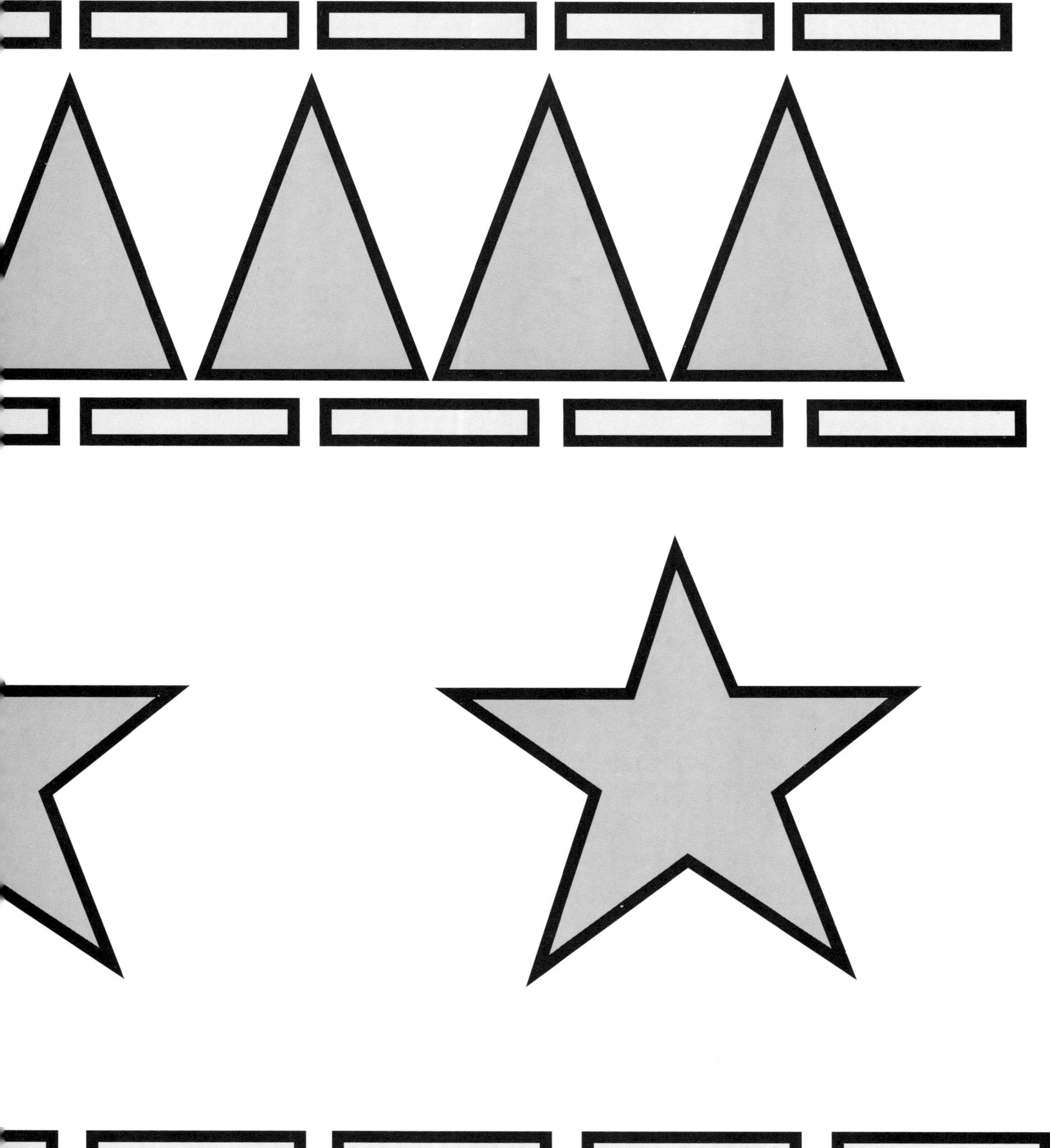

4 Check that you have re-positioned the newspaper masking the areas you do not wish to spray, taking special care to cut and position pieces under the stencil where the overlaps occur.

5 Re-shake the aerosol and apply a light coat of spray. Leave to dry and then repeat.

6 The floor will need to be sealed with appropriate varnish; polyurethane floor varnish is durable. Work in a well-ventilated area and wear a vapour mask if necessary. A minimum of three coats will be necessary, more for areas which get a lot of wear; follow manufacturers' instructions and make sure to sand between each coat when thoroughly dry or the varnish will be inclined to flake off with wear.

This design looks fresh and modern in black on blonde wood, but would look sophisticated in black or a dark colour on darker or stained wood. It would also be effective on a painted floor in contrasting colours, but would still need to be varnished.

TWO COLOUR STENCIL

The plainest room, with no architectural mouldings, such as a skirting board or dado-rail, can be transformed by the use of quite simple stencil techniques and careful choice of colour. In this project, the 'dado-rail' and 'skirting-board' have been created with paint, using careful measurements and masking tape to achieve the correct proportions and straight lines.

The stencil design was modified from a multi-coloured nineteenth-century wallpaper design. The format of alternating square and diamond shapes was retained, with small links or 'ties' left uncut at intervals in the long straight lines to stop the stencil from becoming too fragile to use repeatedly. Bright, contrasting colours were chosen for a dramatic effect. Three colours were applied, using just two stencils.

Because the vivid blue chosen for the background is considerably darker than the shades of yellow and green applied over it, a sponge was chosen to apply the stencil colours. This gives a mottled, uneven effect of light and shade to the pattern, which adds to its overall vitality.

The colours were applied through the stencil directly over the blue, using two coats for the dark yellow, and one for the light yellow and green. When applying light colours over a dark ground, white can be applied first in order to retain the purity of the stencil colour where a less textured, more regular effect is required.

When stencilling on to a wall the stencil can be attached with masking tape at the upper and lower edges. For a really flat result with minimum paint seepage under the cut edge of the stencil, spray the reverse side of the stencil with spray mount used for graphic layout work. Wait a few seconds until the adhesive is only just tacky, then apply to the wall in the correct position. Remove and repeat after the applied colour is dry.

N.B. Work in a well-ventilated area when using spray adhesive. If necessary, wear a vapour mask.

1 Paint the whole wall with Dulux Definitions matt emulsion 2070-R70B 'Rhythmic' *or* paint the whole wall with a contrasting colour, then measure up 33 in. (82.5cm) from the floor and mark lightly with a pencil. Apply masking tape the entire length of the wall, parallel with the floor. Lay down masking tape on a clean surface and peel off before applying, this helps to avoid spoiling the freshly painted wall. Make sure the lower edge of the tape is firmly pressed down. If you painted the wall with a contrasting colour, paint from the lower edge of the tape to the floor with Dulux Definitions matt emulsion 2070-R70B 'Rhythmic'. Leave to dry thoroughly.

Measure 2 in. (5cm) below the lower edge of the masking tape and apply a second strip parallel with the first. Between the two parallel strips of masking tape paint two coats of Dulux Matchmaker matt emulsion 1184 'Dandelion'.

While you wait for the first coat to dry, measure 6 1/2 in. (16.5cm) up from the floor and apply the lower edge of a third strip of masking tape, as above, parallel with the floor. Apply two coats of Dulux Matchmaker matt emulsion 1184 'Dandelion'. Leave to dry.

2 Copy the patterns supplied on pages 32–3 on to stencil card and cut out with a craft knife.

3 Position the square motif stencil centrally between the yellow 'dado-rail' and 'skirting board' and secure. The horizontal lines on this stencil make it easier to get it straight than in the case with the diamond motif. It is most important to get the first stencil straight, as all the rest will continue at the same angle.

Wearing rubber gloves, apply Dulux Matchmaker matt emulsion 1184 'Dandelion' with a sponge. Allow to dry, leaving the stencil in position. When the first coat is dry, apply a second coat with the sponge.

4 Remove the 'square' stencil and position the 'diamond' stencil, using the two small cut-out shapes in the corners to line up with the corresponding parts of the 'square' stencil already applied. Secure the stencil. With a clean piece of sponge apply Dulux Matchmaker matt emulsion 1181 'Daffodil' to the central leaf motifs **only**. Allow to dry leaving the stencil in position. Then, with a clean piece of sponge apply two coats of Dulux Matchmaker matt emulsion 1184 'Dandelion' to the straight sides of the diamond shape **only**. Omit the leaf shapes. Leave the stencil in position and allow to dry.

5 With a fresh piece of sponge apply Dulux Matchmaker matt emulsion 1239 'Glade' over the pale yellow on the leaf motifs **only**. (Take care not to overlap on to the dark yellow straight lines.)

6 On an offcut of stencil paper cut a circle 3 in. (7.5cm) in diameter, using a compass or by drawing around a cup or other similar round object. Cut out and position by eye in the centre of the 'square' design.

7 Apply one coat of 1181 'Daffodil' and allow to dry with stencil in position. Apply a second coat of 1239 'Glade' and allow to dry. Remove the stencil and re-position on the centre of diamond shape, applying two coats of 1184 'Dandelion'. Repeat around the room. You may need to cut a separate stencil for each corner which can be modified to fit.

8 The colours chosen here give this pattern a flamboyant, modern feel, and the scale of the design makes it very dramatic. However, a more subtle effect could be achieved by using pale, toning colours on a pale background. Dark colours, such as a dark red or mottled brown background, possibly marbled or woodgrained with the stencil applied in shades of muted green, would make the design seem more rich and sombre, creating a rather old-fashioned effect.

STENCILLING ON FABRIC

This project was inspired by a Florentine design of gold *fleur-de-lys* – the emblem of the city – on walls painted an intense blue which had then faded over the centuries. This project shows you how to paint a big, coloured background as well as how to cut a simple, symmetric stencil which can then be repeated on fabric. It is difficult to paint a background so that the colour is completely even with no streaks. Generally it is best to aim for results which are enhanced by the irregularities of the coloured background, which is frequently more lively and has more depth than a perfectly even ground. If you do want perfectly even coloured backgrounds, then silk particularly, as well as cotton, are available in a range of beautiful, commercially dyed, colours which can be an inspiration in themselves.

If you are prepared to paint your own backgrounds, however, you can choose exactly which colours to use, mixing them wet-on-wet as you proceed. Silk was chosen for use with dye, a combination which gives a real intensity to the colour. However, dyes must be steamed to fix them when used in this way. If steaming the silk

to fix it is impractical (it will remain susceptible to the effects of water until steamed) you might choose to use a silk paint which only requires to be ironed for fixing. Javana colours for silk would be preferable as they are reasonably translucent and unthickened. Thickened opaque textile pigments are unsuitable for this project.

Two shades of blue were used to imitate the faded nature of the walls in the reference picture. Specially designed stencil creme was used for the gold effect. This has a crumbly texture, ideal for stippling through the stencil. It is available in a wide range of colours, including metallics.

1 Before starting, you should make sure that the floor and wall against which you will be working is protected with plastic sheeting (see step 4).

Stretch approximately 5 ft. (1.5m) of taffeta on a large frame. Fill an enamel dish with water and pour some dye for painting on silk (Dupont Canard 2009) into another. Wearing rubber gloves and an apron or overalls, apply a weak solution of dye to the silk, dipping a 4 in. (10cm) bristle decorators' brush alternately into the water and a tiny amount of dye. Use strong, rhythmic brush strokes from top to bottom of the silk and then back up to the top. Repeat this until the whole silk is flooded with a wash of pale colour. It is important to keep painting while the silk is wet. Don't leave it to dry when you are halfway across, because you will get a pronounced streak where the dye has dried (unless, of course, that is the effect you want).

2 While the dye is still wet from the first step, pour some Dupont Côte d'Azur (2010) into another enamel dish and repeat step 1 using this darker blue with the turquoise and the water used in step 1.

3   Repeat the layers, building up the proportion of dye to water as you go. Because of the stiff bristles on the decorators' brush you can build streaks of darker colour into the background as you go, if you wish. The final effect is up to you.

4   The finished background will have a wonderful depth and intensity of colour. Note how much mess there is on the floor now. The plastic sheeting mentioned at the beginning really is necessary. The wall behind will get traces of dye on it, too, and so will you, so it is most important that you wear gloves and protective clothing. Leave the silk to dry; steam in a pressure cooker; rinse in cold water; wash in warm soapy water, then rinse again, dry and iron on the wrong side.

N.B. *Once used for textile steaming the pressure cooker should never be used for food again.* Pin the silk to a piece of calico; roll up so that the calico protects the silk from transferring colour during steaming. Roll in aluminium foil and lightly crumple each end. Bend into a crescent shape and place in the basket, inside the pressure cooker. Add water. Secure the lid and steam on lowest pressure for 45 minutes (water volume and pressure as per the manufacturer's instructions).

5 To cut the symmetrical *fleur-de-lys*, fold a piece of paper measuring 8x7 in. (20.5x18cm) lengthways down the centre. Using a pencil, sketch in one half of the *fleur-de-lys*.

6 The fold acts as the axis of symmetry so you only have to draw one half of the *fleur-de-lys*.

7 Cut around the shape of the half *fleur-de-lys* you have drawn. The finished *fleur-de-lys* should be about 6½ in. (16.5cm) in height.

8   On tracing paper draw a grid of rectangles, each measuring 6x6½in. (15x16.5cm). On one row of the grid – horizontally – trace around the *fleur-de-lys* four times in four separate rectangles, each time positioning the *fleur-de-lys* in the centre of the rectangle. Repeat the process three times on the row below. This time place the centre of the *fleur-de-lys* on a vertical line so that the designs on the new line are positioned between those on the line above.

9   Trace the repeated pattern of *fleur-de-lys* on to stencil paper or strong brown wrapping paper. Place the stencil paper on a cutting board and cut around the *fleur-de-lys* shapes with a craft knife.

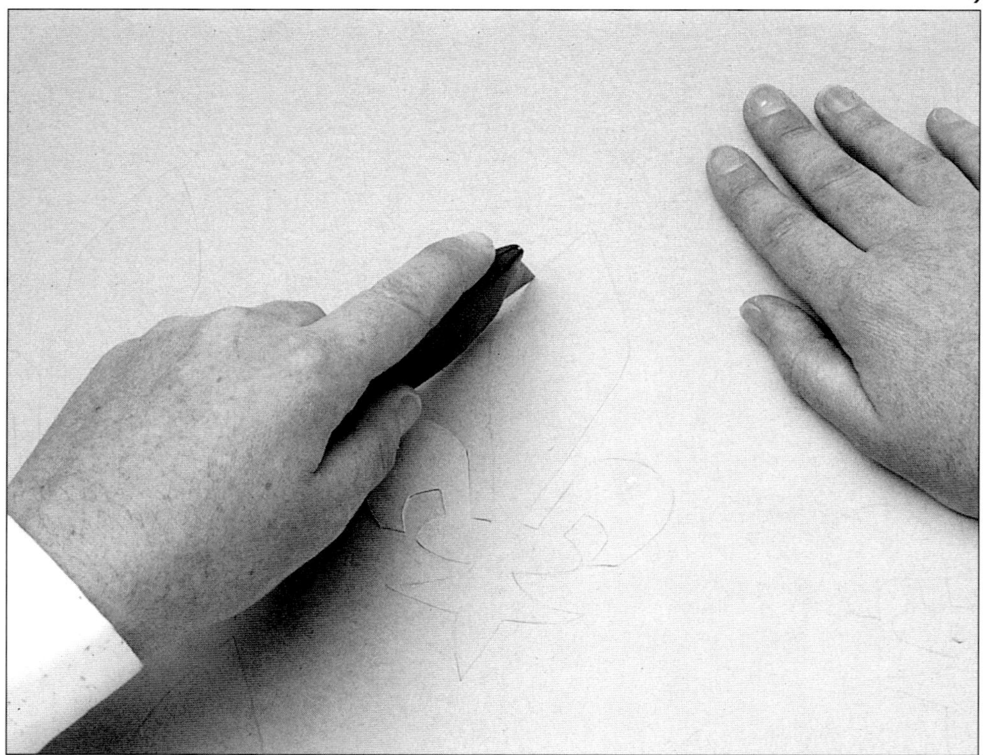

10 When you have finished cutting the *fleur-de-lys,* cut the more complicated scroll border on a separate piece of paper, using the picture as a guide.

11 Place a piece of underfelt or an old blanket on a flat surface – table or large board – and tape it into place with masking tape. Secure the silk background – now fixed, washed and ironed – to the underblanket with double-sided adhesive tape.

Lay the stencil border on the silk in a central position approximately 6 in. (15cm) from the bottom of the silk. Secure it at the corners with masking tape. Using a medium-sized stencil brush, apply gold stencil creme using the brush upright and making short, sharp downward dabs onto the silk. You can vary the depth of shade by applying differing layers of the creme as you go.

12 Check that you have filled in the whole stencil shape before you move on to the next one and then check again when you have finished. Carefully remove the stencil paper, lifting straight up by the edges to avoid smudges. The stencil creme takes up to 24 hours before it is completely dry, but it is possible to continue building up the stencils immediately, as long as you are very careful not to pull the stencil paper across the newly painted surface and smudge it.

13 Position the *fleur-de-lys* stencil carefully above the scroll pattern and lower it gently on to the cloth, taking care of the scroll border. Secure the corners of the stencil paper with masking tape and proceed as at step 11. Repeat as necessary. The bottom part of the scroll of the border can be used on its own as vertical and top borders and the large scrolls can each be filled in with a *fleur-de-lys*.

14 Once you have got used to positioning the stencils accurately, and become confident about working over and around the parts that are still wet, then this becomes a very simple and direct method to use on fabric, so long as you have sufficient space to lay out the full piece of fabric on which you are working. Putting several elements of a repeating pattern on one piece of stencil paper can make registration much faster and simpler, and the combination of lustrous silk, a rich coloured background and gold can make quite grand effects. Thickened textile pigments or dye can be used to apply stencils on fabric, but check manufacturer's instructions to fix them properly.

Ingredients

To Create Each Stencil
2B and HB pencils
Tracing paper
Stencil paper
Craft knife
Board
Masking tape

Cupboard Stencil
Dulux Matchmaker matt
    emulsion 1181 'Daffodil'
    and 1239 'Glade, 250mls
    of each
Small and large stencil
    brushes

Christmas Card
Coloured cartridge paper
3 or 4 saucers or enamel
    dishes
Small sponge
Green, red, black and white
    artists' acrylic paints

Floor Border
Ruler
Lots of old newspapers
Black aerosol paint – several large cans depending on the
    floor area to be covered
Vapour mask (if spray paint used, alternatively you may
    use your
    preferred
    paint)
Floor varnish
Double-sided
    tape

Dado Frieze
Masking tape **or** spray mount (plus a vapour mask if
    spray mount is used)
Dulux Definitions matt emulsion 2070-R70-B Rhythmic
Dulux Matchmaker matt emulsion 1184 'Dandelion',
    1181 'Daffodil' and 1239 'Glade', 250mls of each
Ruler
Sponges
Decorators' brushes, 4 in. (10cm) and 2 in. (5cm)
Compass or a round object approximately 3 in. (7.5cm)
    in diameter

Fleur-de-lys
Unbleached taffeta 5x3 ft (1.5x0.9m)
Fabric frame
Rubber gloves and
    apron
Enamel dishes
4 in. (10cm)
    decorators'
    bristle brush
Stencil brush
Dye for silk (e.g.
    Dupont Canard
    2009, Cote
    d'Azur 2010)
Gold stencil creme